GO, LOVE
and Other

In a rose garden on a warm summer night, a father waits for his daughter to come home. He watches, and waits, and worries . . .

Under a stormy, daffodil-yellow sky, a man returns to his home town after many years away. He walks slowly along a street, remembering the girl he loved, and lost . . .

Among high mountains, in a place where water from a lake thunders over a dam, three people meet – a mother, a daughter . . . and the man who comes between them.

These three stories show us how love grows and changes, like a flower opening and dying, like a storm driving clouds across the sky. They show us how love goes hand in hand with fear and hate and jealousy, and how a moment of madness can change people's lives for ever . . .

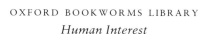

OXFORD BOOKWORMS LIBRARY
Human Interest

Go, Lovely Rose
and Other Stories
Stage 3 (1000 headwords)

Series Editor: Jennifer Bassett
Founder Editor: Tricia Hedge
Activities Editors: Jennifer Bassett and Alison Baxter

Go, lovely rose!
Tell her, that wastes her time and me,
That now she knows,
When I resemble her to thee,
How sweet and fair she seems to be.

———

Go, Lovely Rose!
Edmund Waller (1606–1687)

Go, Lovely Rose

and Other Stories

Retold by
Rosemary Border

OXFORD UNIVERSITY PRESS

OXFORD
UNIVERSITY PRESS

Great Clarendon Street, Oxford OX2 6DP

Oxford University Press is a department of the University of Oxford.
It furthers the University's objective of excellence in research, scholarship,
and education by publishing worldwide in

Oxford New York

Auckland Cape Town Dar es Salaam Hong Kong Karachi
Kuala Lumpur Madrid Melbourne Mexico City Nairobi
New Delhi Shanghai Taipei Toronto

With offices in

Argentina Austria Brazil Chile Czech Republic France Greece
Guatemala Hungary Italy Japan Poland Portugal Singapore
South Korea Switzerland Thailand Turkey Ukraine Vietnam

OXFORD and OXFORD ENGLISH are registered trade marks of
Oxford University Press in the UK and in certain other countries

Original stories © Evensford Productions Ltd

This simplified edition © Oxford University Press 2008

Database right Oxford University Press (maker)

First published in Oxford Bookworms 1989

2 4 6 8 10 9 7 5 3

ISBN 978 0 19 479118 2

Printed in Hong Kong

ACKNOWLEDGEMENTS

Oxford University Press is grateful to Laurence Pollinger Ltd
on behalf of Evensford Productions Ltd for permission
to simplify the three strories in this book.

Illustrated by: Jason Cockcroft

Word count (main text): 8065 words

For more information on the Oxford Bookworms Library,
visit www.oup.com/bookworms

CONTENTS

Go, Lovely Rose

'But who is she with?' said Mr Carteret. 'A young man. She met him on the aeroplane,' Mrs Carteret said. 'Now go to sleep.'

Outside the bedroom window the moon was shining brightly.

'Nobody told me there was a young man on the aeroplane,' said Mr Carteret crossly.

'You saw him,' Mrs Carteret said. 'He was there when you met her at the airport.'

'I don't remember,' said her husband.

'Yes, you do. You noticed his hat. You said so. It was a light green . . .'

'Oh dear!' said Mr Carteret. 'That man? But he's too old for her. He must be nearly forty.'

'He's twenty-eight, dear. Now go to sleep.'

'I can't sleep,' said Mr Carteret. 'Three o'clock in the morning and I can't get to sleep.'

'Just lie still, dear, and you'll soon fall asleep,' said his wife.

It was a warm night in July. A gentle wind whispered in the trees outside the bedroom window. It sounded like a car coming. Mr Carteret sat up and listened. But it was only the wind.

1

'*I can't sleep,*' said Mr Carteret.

'Where are you going now?' said Mrs Carteret.

'I'm going downstairs for a drink of water. I can't sleep. I can never sleep in moonlight – I don't know why. And it's very hot too.'

'Put your slippers on,' said Mrs Carteret sleepily.

He found his slippers and put them on. He went down to the kitchen and turned on the tap. The water was warmish. He let the water run until it was cool enough to drink. Then he opened the kitchen door and went out into the garden. The moon shone on his roses. Mr Carteret could see the shape and colour of every flower. There they were: red and yellow and white, very soft and sweet-smelling. Each flower was wet with dew.

He stood on the short green grass and looked up at the sky. The moon was very bright. It was like a strong, white electric light shining down on the garden.

The wind whispered again in the trees. Again Mr Carteret thought it was a car coming. Suddenly he felt helpless and miserable.

'Sue,' he said aloud, 'Sue . . . where are you? What are you doing? Susie, Susie, you don't usually stay out so late.'

Susie. He always called her Susie when he was specially pleased with her. Usually he called her Sue. When he was cross with her, he called her Susan.

He remembered her nineteenth birthday, three weeks before. She was getting ready to fly off to Switzerland for a holiday.

3

'How lovely she is!' everyone said. 'How pretty and grown-up! And she's going to Switzerland all by herself! How wonderful!'

But Mr Carteret did not think his daughter looked grown-up. To him she looked smaller and more girlish than ever. 'Too young to go away by herself,' he thought crossly.

He heard the church clock. Half past three. At that moment he heard the sound of a car. This time he was sure. He could see its lights coming along the road.

'You're late, young lady,' he said to himself. He did not feel miserable any more; just a little cross. He could hear the car coming quickly along the road. Suddenly he began to run towards the house. He did not want her to find him there. He wanted to get back to bed. His pyjama trousers were too long. They were wet with dew. He held them up, like skirts, as he ran.

'This is stupid,' he thought. 'What stupid things parents do sometimes!'

At the kitchen door one of his slippers fell off. He stopped to pick it up, and listened again for the sound of the car. All was quiet. Once again he was alone in the quiet, moonlit garden. His slippers were wet with dew. His wet pyjama trousers felt uncomfortable on his legs.

'It didn't stop,' he thought. He felt cross and miserable again. '*We* always walked home from dances,' he said aloud. 'That was part of the fun.'

Suddenly he felt frightened. He remembered the corner

4

'What stupid things parents do sometimes!'

on the road near his house. 'It's a dangerous corner,' he said to himself. 'There are accidents there every week. What if Susie and this man . . .' He did not want to think about it. It was too awful.

'And who *is* this man anyway? How do I know he's a suitable friend for Susie? Perhaps he's a married man. Or a criminal.'

All at once he had a terrible feeling about this man. 'I felt like this when I saw her getting into the aeroplane,' he thought. 'I had a feeling of . . . of danger . . . accidents.' He was shaking now. He felt cold and sick. 'She's had a crash in that man's car,' he thought. 'I'm sure of it.'

Now he was walking backwards and forwards across the dewy, moonlit grass. 'I'm sure she's had an accident,' he thought. 'In a minute or two the police will telephone – oh dear! oh dear!'

He began to walk up the road in his pyjamas and bedroom slippers. He looked at the sky; there were lines of gold above the tree-tops. The moon was disappearing. It was almost day. 'Oh, where *is* she?' he cried, and he began to run.

A few moments later, he thought he saw a pair of yellow eyes looking at him from the road. He realized that they were the lights of a car. It was standing at the side of the road. He did not know what to do about it. Should he go up to the car, and knock on the window and say, 'Susan, come home'? But there was always the chance that some other man's daughter was in the car.

'And then what will she think of me – out here in my pyjamas?'

He stopped and watched the light of day filling the sky. 'What will the neighbours think if they see me?' he thought. 'I must go home and get to bed. I don't know why I'm worrying like this. I never worried like this when she was little.'

He turned and started to walk home. Just then he heard a car engine. He looked round and saw its lights coming along the road. Suddenly he felt more stupid than ever. There was no time to get away. He could only hide behind a tree. The long wet grass under the tree made his pyjamas wetter than ever.

The car passed him. He could not see who was inside. 'Perhaps it's Susie,' he thought. 'And now I shall have to go home and change my pyjamas.' He started walking again. Then he stopped once more. 'What if it isn't Susie?' he thought. 'What if something really has happened to Susie?'

He felt sick and cold and miserable. The blood seemed to whisper and sing inside his ears. His heart seemed to fill his whole body.

'Oh, Susie,' he whispered, 'Come home safely. Please. . .'

He realized that the car had stopped outside his house. A moment later he saw Susie. She was wearing her long yellow evening dress. 'How pretty she is!' he thought. He heard her sweet, girlish voice calling: 'Goodbye. Yes. Lovely. Thank you.'

'I mustn't let her see me now,' he thought. 'I must keep out of sight. I must go in through the back door. Then I can go upstairs and put on dry pyjamas . . .'

A moment later the car turned and came back along the road towards him. This time there was no chance to hide. For a few miserable moments he stood there with the lights of the car shining in his eyes.

'Look natural,' he said to himself. 'And hope that nobody notices me.'

The car stopped and a voice called out:

'Excuse me, sir. Are you Mr Carteret?'

'I hope you haven't been worried about Susie?'

8

'Yes,' he said. 'I'm Carteret.' He tried to sound cool and unworried.

'Oh. I'm Bill Jordan, sir. I'm sorry we were so late. I hope you haven't been worried about Susie?'

'Oh! No. Of course not.'

'My mother kept us, you see.'

'But I thought you went to a dance.'

'Oh no, sir. We went to dinner with my mother. We played cards until three o'clock. My mother loves cards. She forgot the time.'

'Oh, that's all right. I hope you had a good time.'

'Oh, we had a wonderful time, thank you. But I thought that perhaps you were worried about Susie . . .'

'No, no. Of course not!'

'That's all right then.' The young man looked at Mr Carteret's wet pyjamas and looked away again. 'It's been a wonderfully warm night, hasn't it?' he said politely.

'Terribly hot. I couldn't sleep.'

'Sleep! I must get home to bed!' He smiled, showing beautiful white teeth. 'Good night, sir.'

'Good night.'

The car began to move away. The young man waved goodbye and Mr Carteret called after him:

'You must come and have dinner with us one evening . . .'

'How kind! Yes, please . . . Good night, sir.'

Mr Carteret walked down the road. 'He called me sir,' he thought. 'What a polite young man! I like him.'

He reached the garden. The new light of morning

shone on his roses. There was one very beautiful red rose, newly opened and dark as blood. 'I'll pick it,' he said to himself, 'and take it upstairs for my wife.' But, in the end, he decided to leave it there.

And then suddenly, a bird began to sing.

There was one very beautiful red rose in his garden.

The Daffodil Sky

B ill got off the train, under a stormy, dark yellow sky. Automatically, he went to the railway footbridge. That was always the quickest way to the town. He could save half a mile that way. And then he saw that the footbridge was closed. There was a big blue notice board. 'Danger. Keep Off.'

'This town has changed,' he said to himself.

So he went the long way, past the factories and along the thin black railway line. Soon he came to a pub. In the old days, Bill often stopped there on his way to market.

In those days he used to come into town every week. He brought his fruit and vegetables or, in early spring, his daffodils, and sold them in the market. In the early days, he had brought them in a horse and cart. But soon he had been ready to buy his first car. . .

The walls of the pub were black with smoke from passing trains. Bill went through the glass door and walked up to the bar.

'I'll have a beer, please,' he said.

Two railwaymen were playing cards in one corner of the bar.

Bill paid for his beer. 'I'm looking for a Miss Whitehead,' he said. 'She used to come in here. She used

11

'*I'll have a beer, please,*' Bill said.

to live in Wellington Street and work in the shoe factory there.'

'That was a long time ago,' said the barman. 'They built a new shoe factory ten years ago – outside the town.'

'She used to come in here when Jack Shipley had this pub.'

'Jack Shipley?' said the barman. 'He's been dead nine years now.'

One of the railwaymen looked up from his card game.

'Do you mean Cora Whitehead?' he said.

'That's right.'

'She still lives in Wellington Street with her old Dad.'

'Thanks very much,' said Bill.

He finished his drink and went out. The sky above his head was still that bright, unnatural daffodil yellow. Suddenly he remembered his first visit to this pub. He had called in, many years ago, during a storm, to get a drink of water for his horse and some beer for himself. 'How many years ago was it?' he thought. 'But I still remember everything so clearly.'

His cart had been full of daffodils, he remembered. They were a bright, burning yellow, like the stormy sky now above his head. He was crossing the bridge when he heard thunder. Then the storm came. He did not have time to cover the cart. 'Come on!' he shouted to

his horse. He drove to the pub. He found a dry place
for his horse and cart. Then he ran through the rain
towards the door of the bar.

'Don't knock me over!' said a girl's voice.

'Sorry,' he said.

He had not noticed the colour of the girl's dress.
Perhaps it was blue; he was not sure. But he had
noticed her large, full, red mouth, also her long,
reddish-brown hair and big brown eyes.

He could not open the door because his hands were
wet. She started to laugh. It was a strong, friendly
laugh, not too loud. A moment later the sun came out.
He felt it on his face and neck.

'You're as good as an umbrella on a wet day,' the
girl said.

The door opened at last, and they were inside the
pub. There was a smell of smoke and beer, sandwiches
and warm bodies. But she said, 'There's a smell of
flowers in here. Can you smell it too?'

'I've got a cart full of flowers,' he said. 'Daffodils.
I've been picking them since six o'clock this morning.
I've got the smell of them on my hands.'

He held up his hands for her to smell.

'That's it,' she said. 'What a lovely smell!'

He watched her as she drank her beer. 'She's
beautiful,' he thought. He wanted to be early at the
market by twelve o'clock. But he stayed in the pub
with her until nearly two. Every time he thought about

14

He watched Cora as she drank her beer.

Customers bought all the shining yellow daffodils.

leaving, the thunder crashed and the rain beat against the window again. Then at last the bright daffodil sun came out again.

'I have to go,' he said.

'You'll be all right,' she said. 'You'll sell all your daffodils. You've got a lucky face. People like you are always lucky.'

'How do you know?'

'I bring them luck,' she said. 'I always do.'

And she was right. All that day, and for a long time afterwards, Bill was lucky. That evening was clear and fine. Customers came to the market. They saw the shining yellow daffodils and they bought them all. 'She was right,' thought Bill. 'She did bring me luck.'

Soon Bill sold his horse and cart and bought a car. At first he did not think he had enough money.

'Listen,' she said. 'Frankie Corbett's got an old car that he wants to get rid of. I'll have a word with Frankie. It'll be cheap – you'll see.'

She was right. Bill bought the car very cheaply.

'You see,' she said. 'I bring you luck.'

That summer Bill began to visit the house in Wellington Street. Cora's mother was dead and her father worked all night on the railway. So it was easy for them to spend the night together. Those were happy times. They did not talk much, but they were very happy. She understood him so well.

'Do you know what?' she said sometimes. 'I know

17

when you turn the corner by the bridge. I feel you near me. I know you're coming, every time.'

Bill rented his land from an old man called Osborne. Osborne had a little farm. He had chickens and a few cows and sheep. Most of the land was covered with old fruit trees. In the spring the daffodils grew thickly at the foot of every tree.

'I'm getting old,' Osborne said one day. 'I'd like to go and live with my sister. I'll sell you my farm, cheap. Pay me a deposit and give me the rest of the money later.'

Suddenly Bill saw all his life in front of him like a bright, beautiful carpet. A farm!

That evening he went for a drive with Cora. They stopped in a field full of summer flowers. The long grass hid them from the road. He lay on his back among the flowers. He looked up at the bright blue sky and talked to Cora about his plans. But Cora was not sure.

'How do you know that this Osborne man is honest?'

'I know Osborne. He's as honest as the day is long.'

'Yes, and some days are longer than others,' she said. 'Don't forget that.'

She looked thoughtfully at him with her big, soft brown eyes.

'How much money have you got?' she asked.

'I've saved a hundred and fifty pounds.'

18

'So you pay Osborne your hundred and fifty pounds as a deposit, and then what do you get?'

'The land. The farm buildings. The animals. The fruit trees. Everything.'

'I don't know,' she said. She lay there for a long time, and looked up at the August sky. Then she shut her eyes, and turned her face towards his. Softly and lovingly they kissed.

After a long time she opened her eyes again. 'I've been thinking,' she said. 'Can I join you in this business? I've got fifty pounds. How much does he want for his farm?'

'A thousand.'

'And we've got two hundred. Can you borrow any more?'

'I don't know where I can get it from.'

'I can get it,' said Cora. 'I'll ask Frankie Corbett. He's got plenty of money – I'll talk to Frankie and ask him to help us.'

Suddenly he was holding her face in his hands. 'We'll get married,' he said. 'You know what you said – you bring me luck.'

They kissed again.

'I'll never forget this day,' thought Bill. 'I feel lucky – the luckiest man in the world. I've got a car, and a house, and a farm . . . and the woman I love.'

'And it all started,' he said aloud, 'with the daffodils.'

'That's how all important things start,' said Cora. 'With something small like a few daffodils. Kiss me again, Bill.'

Six weeks later, on a rainy October evening, he was killing Frankie Corbett . . .

He thought about Frankie Corbett now, as he walked slowly and heavily up Wellington Street, along the rows of smoke-blackened little houses. The sky above the factory chimneys was still dark and stormy.

A man walked up the street with two thin, long-legged dogs beside him. 'That was how Frankie Corbett came that evening,' he remembered. 'But he only had one dog. I knew who he was, because of the dog.'

'Were you waiting for this man?' they had asked him afterwards, all those years ago. But he had only wanted to talk, he told them. That was all. He knew that Frankie Corbett took his dog for a walk every evening. He knew it was a little white, noisy dog. Cora had told him about it.

Bill had not realized how jealous he was. It was not a hot, quick, sudden kind of jealousy. His jealousy was quiet and slow-burning, but it was very strong and deep. It had begun with little things. It started when Cora began to talk about 'Frankie'. 'Frankie will get the money. No, I can't see you tonight because I have to see Frankie.'

He began to feel unsure about her. 'How long have
you known this Frankie?' he asked her.

'Oh, I've known Frankie all my life.'

He was worried now. 'Have you . . . ?' He stopped.

He thought about Frankie Corbett now, as he walked up the street.

21

She knew what he meant, of course. She always understood him so well.

'Oh, we've had a bit of fun sometimes.'

'But . . . is he . . . more than a friend?'

'Oh, we went out together a few times. But we argued all the time. We were no good for each other. He's nothing to me now. But Frankie will do anything for me.'

Bill did not like that. 'What will she do for him in return?' he wondered.

Cora was angry. 'Look,' she said. 'We want the money, don't we? But I can't ask for hundreds of pounds, just like that. Now can I? Be patient.'

It took a month to get the money. Long before the end of the month, his heart was full of jealousy. He could feel it growing inside him, and slowly burning his heart away. He no longer dreamed of the house, the farm, the fruit trees or the daffodils. Instead he dreamed of Cora in another man's arms.

Then came the news about Cora's baby. He was terribly afraid that it was Frankie Corbett's child. And that was why he waited for Frankie Corbett that evening.

People passed and saw him waiting there. Then a small white dog came along. It yapped at Bill. He knew it was Frankie Corbett's dog. Then Frankie Corbett came. He was much older than Bill. He was carrying a walking-stick.

'I can't stand here in the rain, and talk to you,'
said Frankie Corbett.

Bill stopped him. He was shaking violently. 'I must talk to you!' he said thickly. Black and red lines danced in front of his eyes.

It began to rain. 'I'm getting wet,' said Frankie Corbett. 'I can't stand here in the rain, and talk to you.'

'I want an honest answer. That's all,' said Bill. Just then the dog yapped again, and Frankie Corbett lifted his stick angrily.

Suddenly Bill thought that Frankie Corbett meant to hit him with the stick. A minute later Bill was hitting out with his knife. It was a long, thin knife. Bill used it to cut his vegetables. Frankie Corbett fell down and hit his head on the ground.

Cora was right: it was the little things that were

important. The knife, the yapping dog, the people who saw him waiting in the rain. And then, of course, there was his jealousy. At the trial they talked a lot about jealousy.

'How can you describe this man's jealousy?' they asked Cora.

'Black jealousy,' said Cora at once. Bill knew that it was true. She always knew how he felt about things. She loved him truly. But her words had sent Bill to prison for eighteen years . . .

84 Wellington Street. Bill was outside the house now. Above his head the stormy sky was getting darker. He heard the crash of thunder, a long way away. His heart was beating fast, and red and black lines danced in front of his eyes. 'I felt like this when I was waiting for Frankie Corbett,' he thought. 'Will she be there? And if she is there, what can I say to her after all this time?'

He knocked on the door. A light came on inside the house. The door began to open. His heart was beating harder than ever. He waited. A girl stood on the doorstep.

'She hasn't changed,' he said to himself. He remembered the day when they met, the day of the daffodils. 'I loved her then,' he thought, 'and I still love her now.'

'Yes?' she said.

The voice was different. It was quieter and lighter. And then he saw her face, and suddenly he knew. . .

'Are you Cora's daughter?' he asked.

'Yes.'

'I'm an old friend of hers . . . When will she come back?'

'Not until late tonight. She's working at the shoe factory.'

'I see,' he said heavily.

Suddenly the thunder crashed and the rain began to fall.

'Come in,' she said. 'Come in and wait until the rain stops.'

'No, I'll get a bus to the station,' he said.

But the rain was coming down like a waterfall.

'You can't go out in this,' she said. 'Stand here in the doorway.'

His heart was beating violently. The blood seemed to sing in his ears. Her eyes were brown and soft and kind, just like Cora's.

She said, 'Do you have to catch a train? If you don't, perhaps I can lend you an umbrella. You can bring it back tomorrow.'

He looked at the sky above the factory chimneys. 'It looks brighter over there,' he said.

'Wait one more minute,' the girl said. 'Then if the rain doesn't stop, I'll go and get that umbrella.'

He waited, and watched her face. 'Are you still at school?' he asked.

'Oh no! Not me. I work at the shoe factory too. But I work in the daytime.'

25

Suddenly he was afraid to say any more. 'She's going to ask my name,' he thought, but he was afraid to tell her.

'I must go,' he said. 'I don't want to keep you standing here.'

'I'll get the umbrella,' she said.

Suddenly he remembered her mother's words: 'You're as good as an umbrella on a rainy day.'

Then the girl said:

'I'll walk as far as the bridge with you. It isn't raining very hard now. You can get a bus there and I can bring the umbrella back.'

'I don't want to trouble you . . .'

'Oh! That's all right.' She laughed. Her laugh, too, was like her mother's.

She ran out, and held the umbrella over them both. By accident he touched her arm, and felt almost sick with excitement.

'Why are you hurrying?' she asked suddenly. 'Are you going anywhere special?'

She was right. He was hurrying. The excitement of her nearness was driving him on, through the rain. He laughed.

'Nowhere special,' he said.

'I knew it all the time.'

That was like her mother too. He remembered Cora's words: 'I know when you're coming . . . I feel you near me.'

The rain stopped before they reached the bridge. The

26

The rain stopped before they reached the bridge.

sky looked newly washed after the storm. They stood together under that daffodil sky.

'I like being with you,' she said. 'Do you feel like that about some people? You know immediately when you meet them.'

'That's right,' he said.

Suddenly, he wanted to tell her who he was. He wanted to tell her all about himself. He wanted to tell her about her mother, and his lost dream. But he was afraid.

'I can't stay here,' he thought. 'I ought to get out now. I ought to find a little farm like Osborne's, and work there and save my money. I ought to start all over again. There's plenty of farm work at this time of year.'

Then he felt a sudden, awful loneliness. He felt sick and miserable and terribly afraid. He looked up at the yellow sky. 'Will you . . .' he began.

A train went under the bridge with a noise like thunder, and his words were lost. When it had gone, she said, 'What did you say?'

'It doesn't matter. I was just wondering . . . Perhaps you'd like to have a drink with me?'

She smiled. 'Well, what are we waiting for then?'

'Nothing,' said Bill.

They walked together towards the pub. She shook the umbrella and closed it. She looked up at the calm, rain-washed daffodil sky.

'The storm's over,' she said. 'It'll be a lovely day tomorrow.' She smiled again, and he knew she was right.

The Dam

~~~

1

It was September, and of course it was still summer. But sometimes there was snow on the mountains above the lake. It was soft, light snow, like sugar on a cake. And it soon disappeared in the hot sun.

At the bottom of the hotel garden, grape vines grew up a sunny wall. The grapes were small, purple-black and wonderfully sweet.

Every morning, at ten o'clock, a German woman of about fifty came to the garden with a sketch book. She sat under the grape vines and sketched until twelve o'clock. She was tall, straight and serious, with long fair hair and ice-blue eyes. Before she began sketching, she always picked some grapes. Then she ate these slowly, one by one. Her full lips opened and closed around each grape.

'Like kissing,' thought George Graham as he watched her. The woman's warm, full lips seemed so different from the rest of her face. It was like watching two different people: one cold and serious, the other warm and full of fun.

Before twelve o'clock a cold wind began to blow from the west. It blew the woman's papers away. George Graham jumped up from his chair and caught them.

*At the bottom of the hotel garden, grape vines
grew up a sunny wall.*

She smiled – with her lips, not her eyes – and said in careful English:

'I am very grateful.'

'The wind is strong this morning,' he said.

'Yes. I hope it is not going to rain.'

'Usually we have good weather here until November,' said Graham.

'So this is not your first visit?'

'I've been here twice before.'

'So? Well, it is very beautiful,' the woman said.

Then Graham looked at the woman's sketch. To his surprise it did not show the lake or the mountains. Instead, he saw a picture of a girl's face.

'Please do not look at my work,' the woman said. 'It is no good. I only do it to pass the time.'

'But . . . why are you sketching something that isn't there?'

'I am no good at lakes or mountains. I find them boring.'

'May I ask who is the girl?'

'My daughter.'

'Of course. She looks like you.'

She put a grape into her mouth and ate it slowly. Her mouth smiled but her eyes were still cold and unfriendly. Suddenly the sun disappeared. A cold wind blew. 'It isn't very nice out here now,' she said.

'No. It's too cool for sitting. I think I shall go for a drive this afternoon. Have you seen the big new dam that

'*May I ask who is the girl?*' *said Graham.*

they've built at the top of the valley? It's really wonderful.'

'No. I have not seen it.'

'You really ought to see it. Perhaps you would like to come and see it with me this afternoon?'

She put another grape into her mouth and looked at him with those cold blue eyes.

'That is very kind of you,' she said at last. 'I would like to come.'

2

'There isn't much water coming down at this time of year,' said Graham.

They were beside the dam. Its thick grey wall filled the valley. To Graham the dam looked like a big, empty theatre, which was waiting for something exciting to begin. There was no wind now. Everything was very quiet. Their voices sounded unnaturally loud.

'Shall we leave?' she said suddenly. 'I . . . I don't like looking down.'

'You don't like high places? I'm the same.'

'But you come to look at the dam.'

'It interests me,' said Graham. 'I never get tired of looking at it.'

They went back to the car. They got in and the German woman said:

'Where does the road go to?'

The thick grey wall of the dam filled the valley.

'Nowhere. There's a village a few miles up the valley. The road stops there.'

He started the car and they drove up the new, well-made road.

'If it gets cold, we can go into the little restaurant and have hot coffee,' said Graham. 'They have very good cakes there too.'

The woman did not answer. Soon the conversation died. Graham wondered what to say next. Finally he asked:

'How old is your daughter?'

'Trudi is twenty-five.'

'Trudi . . . And what is *your* name?'

'Gerda. Gerda Hauptmann.'

'My name's George Graham. You and your daughter are very much alike.'

'Do you think so? Well, you will be able to see for yourself when she arrives next week. That is, if you are still here then.'

'Yes. I shall be here.'

Twenty minutes later he stopped the car in the village at the head of the valley. They began to walk up the mountain. The weather was changing. It was becoming hot and sunny. Soon they stopped to rest. She sat on a rock and looked around. Her fair hair shone in the sunlight. She looked younger and more attractive than before.

'So you don't like high places?' he said.

'When I was younger I did a lot of mountain-climbing, but I always felt . . .'

'I know,' he said, and took her hand. She looked at him coldly.

'Who said you could do that?'

'Sorry,' said Graham. 'I find you very attractive.'

She looked down at the ground.

'Well, you don't need to worry. My husband is dead,' she said.

'But you are still young and attractive. Don't you feel lonely sometimes . . . ?'

'That is natural.'

'Then let me kiss you.'

She stood up suddenly. 'Not today,' she said. 'I am sorry. But not today.'

Twice in the next four days they walked up the mountain. Twice on the way back they stopped at the little restaurant in the village and had cakes and dark red wine. On the second visit she said:

'Trudi will be here tomorrow – if she doesn't miss the train. She will probably forget to get out at Domodossola.'

'I can drive you to Domodossola to meet her.'

'Oh, let her take the bus,' she said impatiently. 'It will do her good.'

On the way back to the hotel she was warmer, more attractive than ever before. There was a gentle, loving look in her blue eyes.

'Look at that little stone bridge,' she said suddenly.

Soon they stopped to rest. She sat on a rock and looked around.

'What is on the other side? I've always wondered.'

'Well, let's go and see,' said Graham. He stopped the car and they walked across the bridge. On the other side was a forest. A small wooden building stood among the trees. They sat on the seat inside the building. Again he could feel how warm and friendly she was. He touched her arm. She turned her face towards him, and they kissed.

'That was a very beautiful kiss,' she said softly. 'Shall we do it again?'

3

Next morning they drove to Domodossola to meet her daughter. She did not seem excited about it.

'I don't know why we are doing this. She is probably still in Munich.'

'Well, we shall soon know.'

'She is a stupid, thoughtless girl.'

Five miles later, she spoke again.

'I ought to warn you – she doesn't speak very good English.'

'Not like you, then. Where did you learn your English?'

'I had a good teacher.'

The train was not late, and Trudi was on it. Graham saw a tall girl in a fashionable yellow dress. She was

Trudi was like her mother, but much more attractive.

carrying a small blue suitcase and she looked happy and sure of herself. Yes, she was like her mother, but much more attractive.

The two women did not kiss. They did not shake hands. They did not look pleased to see each other.

'Not like a mother and daughter,' thought Graham.

'This is Trudi, Mr Graham,' said Gerda.

'I am pleased to meet you, Mr Graham,' said Trudi.

'May I carry your suitcase?'

'That is very kind of you.'

Her English was excellent. Again he was surprised. He put the suitcase in the boot of the car and held the back door open for her.

'Do you mind if I sit in the front?' she asked politely. 'I get car-sick if I sit in the back.'

'Of course.'

Gerda got into the back and shut the door with a bang.

As he started the engine, Graham said, 'I didn't enjoy that busy road. Shall we go back along the lake? What do you think, Mrs Hauptmann?'

'Please do what you wish,' was the cold reply.

As they drove along, the girl talked happily in her excellent English. Her mother in the back of the car did not say a word.

When they reached the hotel, Graham said, 'Will you both have a drink with me before lunch?'

'Not for me, thank you,' said the mother. 'I am a little tired.'

'Yes, please,' said the girl.

Without another word the mother left them.

In the bar the girl turned to Graham. 'I ought to tell you. My name is not Hauptmann.'

He was too surprised to speak.

'It's Johnson. You see, I am half English.'

He thought about that all through lunch. He ate alone. The girl ate alone too. The mother did not appear in the dining-room. After lunch Graham invited the girl to have coffee with him in the garden.

The waiter put the coffee on a stone table under the vines. Many grapes lay on the ground like little blackish-purple eggs.

The girl picked up a grape and ate it, slowly. 'How like her mother she is,' thought Graham as he watched her.

'These grapes are wonderfully sweet,' she said, 'and they smell so lovely.' Her lips were purple now, like the grapes.

Graham said, 'Your mother didn't come to lunch. I hope she isn't ill.'

'You needn't worry about *her*!' said the girl impatiently. Then she said, 'I think I'll lie in the sun. Will you excuse me while I go up and get my sunsuit?'

She came back ten minutes later in a white sunsuit and lay on one of the hotel's sunbeds.

She had a beautiful figure. Graham could not stop looking at her golden-brown body.

'You're very brown,' he said.

'Oh, I work hard at it,' she said. She sat up and took a bottle of oil from her bag. She oiled her face and neck, then her arms and legs. They shone in the sun.

'Will you do my back, please?' she asked politely.

'I'd love to.' Slowly, gently, he oiled her back, and the backs of her legs.

'That's nice,' she said. 'You do it beautifully. . . You know, it's very nice to find someone like you here. The last time I was here, the hotel was full of old people. Bah!'

'I don't understand about your mother. Why is her name Hauptmann when yours is Johnson?'

'She and my father were not married.'

'Oh . . . Sorry.'

'That's all right. It doesn't worry me. I am Johnson because I prefer my father's name . . . He was a news-paperman in Munich before the war – until . . .'

She stopped, and turned over onto her back.

'Go on,' said Graham. 'Until . . . ?'

'Oh! She killed him. That's all.'

'*What?*'

'You can oil my front now, if you don't mind,' said the girl. She gave him a slow, understanding smile. 'Have you been . . . going out with my mother?'

'We're good friends.'

'Don't forget. Her husband is dead now. She gets . . . lonely.'

Gently he oiled her beautiful brown body. Then

42

'Will you do my back, please?' the girl asked politely.

suddenly a shadow fell across her. He looked up, and saw the mother standing there.

'Please excuse me, Mr Graham. But you promised to take me for a drive at four o'clock.'

'She's caught me,' thought Graham angrily. 'I can't get away.' Aloud he said, 'I'll just wash my hands.' Miserably he went into the hotel.

4

As they drove along, Gerda said, 'You are very quiet this afternoon.'

'Sometimes I like being quiet.'

Gerda laughed. 'What has my stupid daughter been saying to you? I must warn you that she tells lies.'

'She's also very attractive. Why didn't you warn me about that?'

'She is a terrible man-eater. She chases men all the time.' Graham did not know what to say. They drove to a small lake and stopped the car there. Gerda got out of the car. She was wearing an attractive yellow dress. She said:

'That girl has broken so many hearts . . .'

'I'm not planning to fall in love with her,' said Graham shortly.

'Love? She doesn't know the meaning of the word.'

He kissed her, but his kisses were cold and unnatural. She turned away.

'You are a different person today,' she said. 'The other day you were so warm and loving . . .' She stopped. Suddenly, violently, he pulled her towards him and covered her lips with kisses. As he did so, he had a strange feeling. The woman in his arms was not Gerda. It was Trudi.

For the next two days he was never alone with the girl. Every time he saw her, the mother appeared too. Then on the third evening he went out, about ten o'clock, to post some letters. It was a warm night full of the smell of flowers.

'Hullo!' said a voice. 'Where have you been?'

The girl was sitting on a wooden seat at the edge of the lake. He sat down beside her.

'I wanted to ask you something,' he said.

'About what?'

'You said a very surprising thing about your mother on your first day here – when we were in the hotel garden. You said that she killed your father.'

'Oh, she didn't shoot him or anything like that. But – in her own way – she killed him.'

'You hate her, don't you?'

She did not answer.

'Tell me about your father,' said Graham.

'I told you. He worked in Munich for an English newspaper before the Second World War. He was happy there. He loved good food, and wine, and good conversation – and Gerda Hauptmann. But he was clever too.

Then she asked suddenly, 'How old are you?'

He knew that a war was coming. He kept his eyes and ears open. He sent reports back to London.'

'And nobody took any notice.'

'How did you know?'

He laughed. 'It's always like that,' he said.

'Then, in August 1939, he decided to go back to London and warn them. And then the trouble started.'

'But the war started in September, not August.'

'I'm not talking about the war. My mother learnt that she was going to have a baby. She also learnt that my father was planning to leave Munich. She was terribly angry. She screamed and shouted.'

'Why didn't she go with him?'

'And leave Germany? Mr Graham, this was Munich in the 1930s.'

'So what did she do? Did she tell the police that he was a spy?'

'Yes. They didn't kill him at once. But he never saw London again.'

There was a terrible sadness in her voice. Suddenly she seemed very young and very much alone. Gently he put his arm around her.

She sat like that for a moment. Then she asked suddenly, 'How old are you?'

Softly he kissed her lips. 'Thirty-eight . . . half-way between you and your mother, really.'

'Oh no!' she said. 'You are much, much nearer to me.'

She covered his face with kisses.

5

At ten the next morning he walked across the garden. Gerda was sketching under the vines and eating the purple-black grapes one by one.

'Good morning,' said Graham politely. 'Where is Trudi?'

'In bed. She was very late last night.'

'She knows about us,' thought Graham. He said:

'We sat by the lake and talked for a long time.'

'And what lies did she tell you this time?'

'Excuse me. I must go and buy a newspaper.'

'I warned you about that girl.'

'I really must go.'

'The day before yesterday you promised to take me for a drive. Have you forgotten?'

'No. I haven't forgotten.'

'What about this afternoon?'

'I'm sorry, I'm going on a boat trip this afternoon.'

'Alone?' But she already knew the answer.

'With Trudi. We're going to Isola Bella.'

'You'll find it very boring.'

He began to walk away, but again she stopped him.

'I'd like to see the dam again. You promised, remember?'

'Yes.'

'Tomorrow, then?'

'Tomorrow. Goodbye.'

'I warned you about that girl,' said Gerda.

He and Trudi had a wonderful boat trip around the lake. They drank cold white wine and watched the sun on the water. On the way back to the hotel they drank red wine and ate thick meat sandwiches. They watched the sun going down over the lake.

'It will be dark when we get back,' he said. 'Too late for dinner.'

'Who cares about dinner? Let's have more wine.'

After another glass of wine he, too, forgot about dinner. 'Who cares?' he said. He touched her arm.

'Not here,' she said softly.

It was very late when they reached the hotel.

'Would you like a walk by the lake?' he asked.

'May I have some more wine?' she replied. They sat under the vines and he rang the bell for the waiter.

They talked and laughed together as they drank the good red wine. After the second glass she picked up the wine bottle.

'I'm taking this upstairs with me,' she said softly. 'Room 247. Don't forget.'

6

It was almost day when he left Trudi. It was after eleven when he came into the garden. Nobody was sketching under the vines. He went to order coffee, and found Gerda sitting there.

'You are very late this morning,' she said coldly. 'You haven't forgotten our trip?'

'I always keep my promises. But it's my last trip with you.'

'Why?'

'I'm leaving tomorrow.'

Her mouth was thin and angry. 'And where are you going? To England?'

'To Venice.' Then he added, 'With Trudi.'

'I warned you about that girl. She tells lies.'

'I am in love with her.'

'Love? She doesn't know what love is!'

'I am in love with her,' he repeated.

'And you are much older than she is.'

'I am also much younger than you.'

'That was unkind and unnecessary.'

For ten minutes neither of them spoke a word. She did not need to speak. All her feelings were in her face: her hate, her jealousy, her terrible loneliness. He spoke at last.

'I hope you will still come with me to the dam. It's my last chance to see it.'

'Perhaps you prefer to go alone.'

'Oh, I'm not going alone. Trudi is coming too.'

Her voice, when she replied, was as cold as the snow on the mountain tops.

'I will come. Is half past two all right for you?'

* * *

She was very straight and serious as she sat down in the back seat. They drove up the valley. They passed the dam and the little stone bridge.

'There's a lot of water coming over the dam today,' said Graham. 'I think it rained during the night. We'll stop and look on the way back. Are you afraid of high places, Trudi?'

'Not at all.'

'Your mother is.'

The two women looked angrily at each other.

'I've said the wrong thing again,' Graham thought.

He stopped the car at the head of the valley. Suddenly the air was cold. Trudi wore only a thin yellow dress. Graham took off his coat and put it around her. 'Here, take this,' he said. Gerda's face was hard and angry.

In the restaurant he asked them what they wanted.

'Coffee,' said Gerda coldly.

'Wine, please,' said Trudi.

He tried to make conversation. He talked amusingly about Venice. Silently Gerda drank her coffee and looked at her daughter with black hate in her eyes.

They drove back towards the dam. He stopped at the little stone bridge.

'Come on. I want to take a photo of the two of you on the bridge.'

'You don't need me,' said Gerda shortly. 'I will stay in the car.'

* * *

He stood on the bridge with Trudi. 'I haven't kissed you today,' he said.

'I know.'

'It was very beautiful last night.'

'Oh yes. Very beautiful.'

He kissed her softly, lovingly.

'That was beautiful too,' she said.

They walked back to the car and drove to the dam.

'I want a photo of the two of you,' said Graham. 'On the wall above the dam.'

To his surprise, Gerda agreed.

'Go up together,' he told them. 'I have to finish this film first. It's black and white, you see. I'll put a colour film in for you two.'

The girl and her mother walked along the high wall above the dam while George Graham walked the other way. Water was falling over the dam with a noise like thunder.

'How beautiful it is,' he thought, 'this wall of water shining in the sun.'

He finished his black and white film and put a colour one into his camera. 'A colourful picture,' he thought. 'Deep blue sky, snow on the mountains, the autumn leaves on the trees. Gerda in her red dress, Trudi in her yellow dress and my green coat. And the white water falling over the dam. A lovely picture.'

And then he heard the scream. Something went past him through the falling water. 'A fish,' he thought.

Then he realized that it was the body of the girl.

High up on the dam, the mother was standing very straight, like a soldier. There was no sign of the girl. There was only the grey wall of the dam and the thunder of the falling water.

The mother was standing very straight, like a soldier.

54

GLOSSARY

attractive pleasing and nice to look at

beer an alcoholic drink, usually light brown in colour

blow (past tense **blew**) when air moves, a wind is blowing

by accident by chance; accidentally

cart *(n)* a kind of car, with two or four wheels, pulled by a horse

daffodil a bright yellow flower that grows in spring

dam *(n)* a wall built across a river to hold water back

deposit *(n)* a first payment for something (the rest of the money is paid later)

dew very small drops of water that cover grass, flowers, etc. during the night

fall in love with to become suddenly very much in love with somebody

grape a small green or purple fruit that grows in warm countries

grown-up adult; no longer a child

impatiently not patient; in a hurry

jealous unhappy and angry because you are afraid of losing someone's love

kiss *(v and n)* to touch someone with your lips in a loving way

line *(n)* a long, thin mark (writing paper sometimes has lines on it)

oil *(n)* a thick liquid made from plants; people put oil on their skin to help it go brown in the sun

oil *(v)* to put oil on something

pyjamas a loose jacket and trousers that people wear in bed

rent *(v)* to pay somebody money to use a house, shop, etc.

rose   a flower with a sweet smell

sight *(n)*   the ability to see; **out of sight** where you cannot see it

sketch *(n* and *v)*   a picture, usually drawn quickly, in pencil

slipper   a soft, comfortable shoe to wear indoors

still   not moving

tap *(n)*   something on the end of a pipe that you turn to let water come out

thought   the act of thinking; something that you think

thoughtless   not thinking of other people and what they would like

thunder *(n)*   a loud noise during a storm that comes after the lightning (a sudden, very bright light)

trial   after someone is arrested by the police, there is a trial to decide if the person must go to prison or not

trip *(n)*   a journey

vine   a climbing plant that grapes grow on

war   fighting between two or more countries

wave *(v)*   to move your hand through the air, usually to say hullo or goodbye to someone

whisper *(v)*   to speak very quietly, or to make a very quiet noise

wine   an alcoholic drink made from grapes

yap *(v)*   to make short, sharp sounds like a little dog

Go, Lovely Rose
and Other Stories

ACTIVITIES

Before Reading

1 **Read the back cover, and the introduction on the first page of the book. What do you think these stories are about? Choose three of these ideas, one for each story.**

1 A man who killed the girl he loved.

2 Two women who want the same man.

3 A man who comes back to look for the girl he loved.

4 A daughter's love for her father.

5 A father's love for his daughter.

6 A mother's love for her daughter.

2 **What can you guess about these three stories? Choose one ending for each of these sentences.**

Go, Lovely Rose

1 The man's daughter is not at home because . . .

a) she is working late at the office.

b) she has gone to a party with some girlfriends.

c) she has gone out with a young man.

2 The father is worrying because . . .

a) his daughter is driving his car and isn't a good driver.

b) his daughter doesn't usually stay out as late as three o'clock in the morning.

c) he knows her friends often do stupid or dangerous things.

The Daffodil Sky

3 The man has been away from his home town because . . .

    a) he has been fighting in a war.

    b) he has been in prison.

    c) he has been working in another country.

4 He lost the girl he loved because . . .

    a) he did something terrible.

    b) she married another man.

    c) she died in an accident.

The Dam

5 The man in this story falls in love with . . .

    a) the mother.

    b) the daughter.

    c) both women.

6 At the end of this story the two people still alive are . . .

    a) the mother and the daughter.

    b) the daughter and the man.

    c) the mother and the man.

3 **Before you read the first story, *Go, Lovely Rose*, can you imagine how the father is feeling? Circle all the words that you think are possible.**

afraid	excited	miserable
amused	happy	pleased
angry	helpless	stupid
ashamed	jealous	tired
bored	lonely	worried

While Reading

Read *Go, Lovely Rose*, and then answer these questions.

Why

1 . . . couldn't Mr Carteret sleep?
2 . . . was he worried about Susie?
3 . . . did he go into the kitchen?
4 . . . did he hide behind a tree?
5 . . . did he like Bill Jordan?
6 . . . do you think he decided not to pick the rose?

Read *The Daffodil Sky*. Put sentences 10 to 18 in the right order, and join them to these beginnings.

1 One stormy spring morning . . .
2 That afternoon, . . .
3 Over the next few months, . . .
4 One summer evening . . .
5 But after a while . . .
6 When Bill learnt about Cora's baby, . . .
7 After eighteen long years in prison . . .
8 When he heard that Cora had not moved away, . . .
9 As soon as the young girl opened the door, . . .

10 Bill became very jealous of Cora's friend Frankie Corbett.
11 Bill met Cora Whitehead outside a railwaymen's pub.
12 Bill returned to the same pub.

13 he sold all his daffodils at the market.

14 they decided to buy a farm together and get married.

15 Bill knew that it was Cora's daughter.

16 he went out and killed Frankie Corbett.

17 Bill and Cora became very close.

18 he went straight to her house.

Read Chapters 1 to 4 of *The Dam* (to the bottom of page 47). Are these sentences true (T) or false (F)? Rewrite the false ones with the correct information.

1 Gerda was tall and fair, with warm brown eyes.

2 She always sat in the hotel garden and sketched the lake.

3 Graham invited Gerda to go with him to see the new dam.

4 On the day before Trudi arrived, Gerda let Graham kiss her for the first time.

5 Trudi was less attractive than her mother.

6 At the station Gerda and Trudi kissed and shook hands.

7 Trudi asked Graham to put sun-oil on her body.

8 Trudi warned Graham that her mother was a man-eater.

9 Trudi told Graham that Gerda had killed her father.

Before you read the end of *The Dam*, can you guess what happens? Choose Y (yes) or N (no) for each sentence.

1 Graham and Gerda become lovers. Y/N

2 Graham and Trudi become lovers. Y/N

3 Trudi and her mother leave the hotel and go away. Y/N

4 Graham takes Gerda and Trudi up to see the dam. Y/N

5 Something terrible happens at the dam. Y/N

61

After Reading

1 **Perhaps this is what some of the characters in the stories were thinking. Which characters were they (two from each story), and who were they thinking about?**

1 'He's the nicest man I've met in a long time. He seems very kind and gentle. And tomorrow he's taking me to Venice! I'm just so happy!'

2 'She's nineteen now. Sensible. Grown-up. She's probably enjoying herself with that nice young man. I'm not going to worry about her, and I'm going back to sleep.'

3 'I couldn't leave an old friend of Mum's standing out there in the rain. He seemed a bit sad and lonely. And I don't know why, but I immediately felt comfortable with him.'

4 'Of course he was worried! There he was, out in the street, in his pyjamas and slippers! But he seemed very pleasant. And it was nice of him to ask me to dinner.'

5 'He wanted to kiss me today, but it was too soon, much too soon. Perhaps I'll let him kiss me in a day or two. He's younger than me, of course, but never mind . . .'

6 'She looks at me with her big brown eyes, and says she wants to borrow eight hundred pounds. I don't know. It's a lot of money. I'll have to think about it . . .'

2 Here are some different titles for the stories. Which ones are suitable for which stories? Explain why. Which titles do you prefer? Can you think of any more?

Jealous Love   Killing for Love
The Smell of Flowers   Just Like Her Mother
The Girl in the Yellow Dress   A Daughter's Smile

3 Perhaps Susie wrote her diary after her night out with Bill Jordan. Choose suitable words to complete this page in her diary (one word for each gap).

I've just had the most _____ evening! Bill Jordan took me to his _____ house for dinner. It was a lovely _____ night, and I wore my favourite _____ evening dress. Bill _____ I looked beautiful! I really like Bill, he's great fun. His mother's nice _____. She _____ a fantastic meal, and then we played _____ for hours. We all had a _____ time – it was three _____ when we finished!

Then Bill _____ me home. But guess what? Just _____ we got to the house, I _____ Dad in the street. He was _____ behind a tree next to the road – in his _____ and slippers! He looked so stupid! I _____ Bill didn't see him . . .

4 Now write Mrs Jordan's diary for the same evening. Think about these questions when you write.

- Did Mrs Jordan enjoy the evening?
- What did she think about her son's new girlfriend?
- Why did they all play cards until so late?

5 **What did Cora say to the police, after Bill's arrest? Write out their conversation in the correct order, and put in the speakers' names. The policeman speaks first (number 5).**

1 _____ 'Is he really? Are you sure about that? Has he never hit *you*, for example?'

2 _____ 'Never. Mm. Well, does he often carry a knife?'

3 _____ 'No, he isn't. He's a gentle person.'

4 _____ 'Yes, he does. In fact, he always carries one.'

5 _____ 'So, Miss Whitehead, tell me about Bill. Is he a violent man?'

6 _____ 'Yes, I suppose he does. Well, would you say that he was a jealous man, then?'

7 _____ 'No, sir. He's never done that. Never.'

8 _____ 'Does he now? And why is that?'

9 _____ 'Yes, sir. I'm afraid I would.'

10 _____ 'Because of his work. He grows flowers, and fruit and vegetables, you see. So he needs to carry a knife.'

6 **Perhaps Cora's daughter and Bill return to the house to meet Cora when she comes home from work. What happens next? Complete these three possible endings (use as many words as you like), and choose the one you like best. Explain why.**

1 As they entered the living room, the first thing that Bill noticed was the smell of flowers.

'Lovely, aren't they?' said the girl. 'Daffodils have always been my mother's favourite flowers.'

Then Bill saw Cora. Their eyes met and _____.

64

2 As they entered the living room, Bill saw a letter lying on the table. On it he read the words 'Miss Corbett'.

'Miss Corbett?' he said. 'Is that . . .?'

'Yes, that's me,' replied the girl. 'I've got my father's name. He died before I was born.'

Bill was silent for a moment, and then _____.

3 As they entered the living room, the girl said, 'Mum, you've got a visitor.'

Cora turned round. Bill saw the same reddish-brown hair, the same full red lips. But her eyes had changed. In her eyes Bill saw eighteen years of pain. At that moment he knew _____.

7 This is what Graham told the police about Trudi's death, but he says several things which are not true. Can you find his lies and correct them?

'The girl's name was Miss Trudi Hauptmann. She was on holiday with her mother, Mrs Gerda Hauptmann. They were very friendly with each other, and spent a lot of time together.

'When we got to the dam, the two women went up on to the high wall because they wanted to look at the mountains. Trudi had said she was afraid of high places, but I don't know what happened. I didn't hear anything, and I didn't see anything. When I looked up at the wall above the dam, I saw Mrs Hauptmann waving at me, and crying.

'No, I was not in love with either of the women, and I spent last night in my own room. In fact, I was planning to leave tomorrow and return to England.'

8 **What do you think Gerda and Trudi said when Graham was not there? Complete Trudi's part of the conversation.**

GERDA: I hope it's not going to happen again, Trudi.

TRUDI: I don't _____.

GERDA: You know very well what I mean. Every time I start seeing a man, you steal him from me.

TRUDI: I'm only _____.

GERDA: Yes, it starts with boat trips. Then it's dinner, then—

TRUDI: You _____.

GERDA: I'm not crazy. I can see what you're doing – the way you look at him, the way you talk to him . . .

TRUDI: Mother, I'm twenty-five, and I can _____.

GERDA: Oh no, you can't. I won't let you see him again.

TRUDI: Oh yes? And what _____?

GERDA: You'll see what I can do, just you wait and see . . .

9 **What did you think about the people in *The Dam*? Do you agree or disagree with these ideas? Explain why.**

1 Trudi *was* a 'man-eater', but Graham couldn't see it.

2 Gerda pushed Trudi over the edge of the dam. She was a crazy woman, and a murderer.

3 Graham was caught in a battle between two women, and what happened was not his fault.

10 **Which of the three stories did you like most, and which did you like least? Explain why.**

ABOUT THE AUTHOR

Herbert Ernest Bates was born in Northamptonshire in 1905. His family were shoe-makers. After leaving school, he spent a short, unhappy time as a newspaper reporter, and then took a job in the office of a shoe factory warehouse. He spent many hours alone in the office, and it was here that he wrote his first novel, *The Two Sisters*, which was published in 1926.

During the Second World War, Bates joined the Royal Air Force. As well as his wartime duties, Bates was employed as the Armed Forces' first short-story writer, writing under the name of 'Flying Officer X'. During this time he published several collections of short stories, including *There's Something in the Air* (1943) and *How Sleep the Brave* (1943). His most famous novel, *Fair Stood the Wind for France* (1944), is about the crew of a British plane shot down in France. In 1945 he was sent to Burma, and his novel *The Jacaranda Tree* (1949) was based on his wartime experiences in that country. After the war Bates travelled widely, writing in Tahiti and many other parts of the world. He died in 1974.

For fifty years H. E. Bates published at least one new novel or collection of short stories every year, and several of the novels have been made into successful films or television serials. Perhaps his best-loved character is Pa Larkin, the happy family man of *The Darling Buds of May* (1958). Bates, like Pa Larkin, lived with his wife and children in the peaceful countryside of Kent; and, like his famous character, is remembered as a passionate Englishman, with a deep love of the countryside and the beauty of nature.

OXFORD BOOKWORMS LIBRARY

*Classics • Crime & Mystery • Factfiles • Fantasy & Horror
Human Interest • Playscripts • Thriller & Adventure
True Stories • World Stories*

The OXFORD BOOKWORMS LIBRARY provides enjoyable reading in English, with a wide range of classic and modern fiction, non-fiction, and plays. It includes original and adapted texts in seven carefully graded language stages, which take learners from beginner to advanced level. An overview is given on the next pages.

All Stage 1 titles are available as audio recordings, as well as over eighty other titles from Starter to Stage 6. All Starters and many titles at Stages 1 to 4 are specially recommended for younger learners. Every Bookworm is illustrated, and Starters and Factfiles have full-colour illustrations.

The OXFORD BOOKWORMS LIBRARY also offers extensive support. Each book contains an introduction to the story, notes about the author, a glossary, and activities. Additional resources include tests and worksheets, and answers for these and for the activities in the books. There is advice on running a class library, using audio recordings, and the many ways of using Oxford Bookworms in reading programmes. Resource materials are available on the website <www.oup.com/bookworms>.

The *Oxford Bookworms Collection* is a series for advanced learners. It consists of volumes of short stories by well-known authors, both classic and modern. Texts are not abridged or adapted in any way, but carefully selected to be accessible to the advanced student.

You can find details and a full list of titles in the *Oxford Bookworms Library Catalogue* and *Oxford English Language Teaching Catalogues*, and on the website <www.oup.com/bookworms>.

THE OXFORD BOOKWORMS LIBRARY
GRADING AND SAMPLE EXTRACTS

STARTER • 250 HEADWORDS

present simple – present continuous – imperative –
can/cannot, must – *going to* (future) – simple gerunds ...

Her phone is ringing – but where is it?

Sally gets out of bed and looks in her bag. No phone. She looks under the bed. No phone. Then she looks behind the door. There is her phone. Sally picks up her phone and answers it. *Sally's Phone*

STAGE 1 • 400 HEADWORDS

... past simple – coordination with *and, but, or* –
subordination with *before, after, when, because, so* ...

I knew him in Persia. He was a famous builder and I worked with him there. For a time I was his friend, but not for long. When he came to Paris, I came after him – I wanted to watch him. He was a very clever, very dangerous man. *The Phantom of the Opera*

STAGE 2 • 700 HEADWORDS

... present perfect – *will* (future) – *(don't) have to, must not, could* –
comparison of adjectives – simple *if* clauses – past continuous –
tag questions – *ask/tell* + infinitive ...

While I was writing these words in my diary, I decided what to do. I must try to escape. I shall try to get down the wall outside. The window is high above the ground, but I have to try. I shall take some of the gold with me – if I escape, perhaps it will be helpful later. *Dracula*

... should, may – present perfect continuous – *used to* – past perfect –
causative – relative clauses – indirect statements ...

Of course, it was most important that no one should see
Colin, Mary, or Dickon entering the secret garden. So Colin
gave orders to the gardeners that they must all keep away
from that part of the garden in future. *The Secret Garden*

*... past perfect continuous – passive (simple forms) –
would conditional clauses – indirect questions –
relatives with *where/when* – gerunds after prepositions/phrases ...

I was glad. Now Hyde could not show his face to the world
again. If he did, every honest man in London would be proud
to report him to the police. *Dr Jekyll and Mr Hyde*

*... future continuous – future perfect –
passive (modals, continuous forms) –
would have conditional clauses – modals + perfect infinitive ...

If he had spoken Estella's name, I would have hit him. I was so
angry with him, and so depressed about my future, that I could
not eat the breakfast. Instead I went straight to the old house.
Great Expectations

*... passive (infinitives, gerunds) – advanced modal meanings –
clauses of concession, condition

When I stepped up to the piano, I was confident. It was as if I
knew that the prodigy side of me really did exist. And when I
started to play, I was so caught up in how lovely I looked that
I didn't worry how I would sound. *The Joy Luck Club*

Love Story

ERICH SEGAL

Retold by Rosemary Border

This is a love story you won't forget. Oliver Barrett meets Jenny Cavilleri. He plays sports, she plays music. He's rich, and she's poor. They argue, and they fight, and they fall in love.

So they get married, and make a home together. They work hard, they enjoy life, they make plans for the future. Then they learn that they don't have much time left.

Their story has made people laugh, and cry, all over the world.

As the Inspector Said and Other Stories

RETOLD BY JOHN ESCOTT

The murder plan seems so neat, so clever. How can it possibly fail? And when Sonia's stupid, boring little husband is dead, she will be free to marry her handsome lover. But perhaps the boring little husband is not so stupid after all . . .

Murder plans that go wrong, a burglar who makes a bad mistake, a famous jewel thief who meets a very unusual detective . . . These five stories from the golden age of crime writing are full of mystery and surprises.